An Introductio...
Princely Armours...
Weapons of Childho...

This book was inspired by an exhibition, *The Knight is Young*, held by the Royal Armouries between autumn 2002 and spring 2004 at the museum's three sites – Leeds, Fort Nelson and the White Tower. The exhibition featured a collection of over 40 weapons and armour made for children between the 15th century and the end of the 19th century.

The Stuart Princes' armour and a set of miniature cannon made for Charles II in 1638–39 form the centrepiece of this fascinating collection. All the fine objects illustrated in this book are from the Royal Armouries' collection and many are outstanding examples of the craftsman's art.

Bridget Clifford

Karen Watts

Bridget Clifford
Senior Curator (Library)
Royal Armouries, Tower of London

Karen Watts
Senior Curator (Armour)
Royal Armouries, Leeds

Contents

Examining the evidence 2
Medieval might 4
Terrific Tudors 10
Sterling Stuarts 16
Honourable Hanoverians 28
Young blades 30
Georgian sharpshooters 32
Virtuous Victorians 34
Modern major general 36
Boyz toyz 38
Oriental *by Ian Bottomley* 44
What no girls! 46
Further reading 48

There has been much academic debate about the nature of childhood and children's experiences in the past. Few children set down accounts of their lives and their innermost thoughts. We can piece together something of the world they lived in from others' reactions to them and those of their possessions which have survived.

Our information about children's arms and armour comes mainly from surviving objects, written accounts and paintings showing them being used. Personal letters, diaries, wills and bills all help us build up a picture of their use and availability.

▲ *Children playing at jousting with hobby-horses and toy windmill-lances.* Border decoration from the Golf Book, Flemish 1520-30. The British Library

Recycling

Trainee knights had to learn their trade, their more workaday equipment was recycled as it became too small, and then finally discarded when it could no longer be adequately repaired.

Boy's weapons probably suffered a similar fate. Sometimes they were updated. This child's sporting gun (XII.330) has had the original 18th-century lock modernised for a new owner in the early 19th century.

Boys' dress swords were very much for best and usually beautifully decorated, but even so few have survived. Practice weapons, whether for children or adults are very rare.

▼ *Child's sporting gun.* XII.330

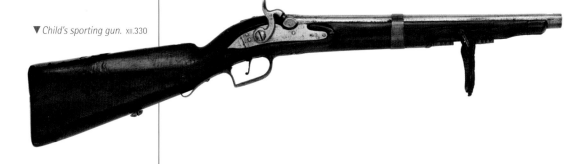

Everyday objects?

All evidence has to be treated with caution. We have to ask why specific pieces survived – are they typical, everyday objects, or were they thought so unusual at the time that special efforts were made to preserve them?

It is difficult to tell how common full suits of armour were for boys. A suit of armour was tailor made to fit its owner and represented a considerable investment. How much more so a boy's armour, soon to be outgrown? Sir John Chamberlain commented rather waspishly in 1608 that Sir Henry Lee presented *'the Prince with an armour that stoode him in 200 li. (£200) and within a yeare or two will serve his turn neither for jest nor ernest'.*

Portraits

Portraits of families were staged to show them at their best. Today we take the camera and camcorder for granted, but without such tools only a very few could afford to record their image for posterity. Great care was taken to make sure that the onlooker was aware of the sitter's social position and wealth. No informal poses here, but a calculated, formal record. Sometimes the arms and armour shown in the picture were props, adapted to emphasise a point. Charles II's boyhood armour (II.90) is apparently worn by his 27-year-old nephew William in a portrait of 1677 (I.40 – see also p.22). William was marrying into the family, and by being shown in his uncle's armour (made for Charles when he was 14) this new alliance was celebrated – with the help of some artistic licence.

▲ *Portrait of William as Duke of Orange, Dutch, about 1677.*
I.40

Children will be children

Faced by shockingly high rates of infant and child mortality, most families got on with the business of living as best they could. Educationalists and philosophers could debate the nature of the child – from 'sinful polluted creatures' (*Evangelical Magazine*, 1799) to Wordsworth's vision of innocents trailing heavenly clouds of glory – the truth lay somewhere between. Bartholomew the Englishman's description of children is equally true for the 13th or the 21st century:

Children often have bad habits, and think only of the present, ignoring the future ...They cry and weep more over the loss of an apple than over the loss of an inheritance. ...They desire everything they see, and call and reach for it ... Suddenly they laugh, suddenly they weep, and are continuously yelling, chattering and laughing.

Most of the aristocracy lived quiet, peaceable lives, but they were all supposed to have weapons and armour and know how to use them. An important part of a boy's education was his training in military skills.

▶ 'The Stages of Life' *from 'Le Livre des Propriétés des Choses' by Bartholomew the Englishman, 1485. École Nationale Vétérinaire, Maisons-Alfort, France.* Archives Charmet/Bridgeman Art Library

The seven ages of man

Medieval people believed that they progressed through a series of phases in their life called the 'stages of life'. This 15th-century woodcut shows the 7 ages: the baby in the crib, the toddler with his walking frame, the child riding a hobby horse with his toy lance aimed at the toddler, a boy of 7, an adolescent of 14, the grown man and finally the old man with his stick.

▲ *Running at the 'human target'* After Joseph Strutt, from *The Romance of Alexander,* Flemish, 1338–44. Bodleian Library, Oxford

Education

Aristocratic children's education, especially that of boys, was considered important, and a number of books on the subject have survived from the Middle Ages. Stories and poems about heroes and saints often included accounts of their early life and training. From the 12th century serious writings on the instruction and training of princes and knights were produced. Many drew on Greek and Roman authors, adapting their theories and concentrating on the ruling elite. Especially popular among the aristocracy were the 'mirrors' or instruction books intended for royalty, but read avidly by the nobility. Advice was offered on conduct and the skills and accomplishments that the growing prince or noble son should be taught. Like modern childcare manuals, it is impossible to tell how widely or closely they were followed, or how far they really reflected practice at the time. Importantly they helped establish aims and methods of education still current today.

Mail shirt, European, early 15th century.
Mail was made of interlocking rings of thick, round-section iron wire. This mail shirt was made with alternate rows riveted (with tiny nail-heads) and welded closed. There are many repairs showing that it was well worn, probably by many different boys. The opening at the front has also been expanded. Padded textile clothes would be worn underneath. III.3282

Bull's eye!

Some teachers managed to combine arms and book learning. The Italian humanist and scholar Erasmus suggested in 1497 that *'a constant element of enjoyment must be mingled with our studies so that we think of learning as a game rather than a form of drudgery'.* He gave the example of an English father who, noting his son's enthusiasm for archery, devised a novel way of teaching him his letters. The boy was given a specially made archery set decorated with the letters of the alphabet, and a target with the Greek and Roman alphabets on it. If he hit the target and correctly pronounced the letter he won a prize. Erasmus commented *'It was by means of this stratagem that the boy in question learnt in a few days of fun and play to identify and pronounce his letters – something which the majority of teachers with all their beatings, threatenings and insults could scarcely have accomplished in three years'.*

Training to be a knight

Brothers and sisters were raised together in the nursery until about the age of 7, when the boys began their training with a male tutor, often in another household. They received a broad education including religious studies, the three Rs (reading, writing and arithmetic), etiquette and physical training.

First of all, they practised fighting on foot with each other using wooden and blunted swords. They learned to get used to wearing armour which, which in the days before plate armour, was usually a mail shirt and a helmet.

▼ *Boys running at the rotating quintain and the fixed target.* After Joseph Strutt, from *The Romance of Alexander*, Flemish, 1338–44. Bodleian Library, Oxford

Lances

Young boys also learned to ride and to control a horse. Controlling a lance is a difficult skill to master. The boys first practised running around with toy lances which had a windmill tip that spun round as it caught in the wind. As they got more practised they used sharp lances and tried to catch rings on the lance tips (called 'running at the ring') and with blunted lances tilted at rotating targets called quintains. The final skill, at about 14 years, was mastering the lance while riding.

Horsemanship

Horses were an everyday part of life and everyone of substance rode unless they were very young or infirm - most children learnt to ride at an early age. Henry, Edward I's second son, was given a white horse of his own in 1274 when he was 7 years old. A century later, Henry IV's sons John and Humphrey were 10 and 12 respectively when their father bought them their first horses.

Playtime

Young boys were encouraged to play with specially made weapons. Nine-year-old King Henry VI received 8 swords in 1430 *'some greater and some smaller, for to learn the king to play in his tender age'.* He also had a little suit of armour decorated with gold made for him. It was to little avail, as Henry grew into a singularly unwarlike adult. He was deposed twice and finally murdered in 1471.

▼ From The Book of Chivalry written by a 14th-century French knight, Geoffroi de Charny.

Key stages

As they grew older aristocratic children were introduced to hunting and archery. Hunting was widely pursued by the nobility and gentry of both sexes. The skills it taught were thought to be good training for war both physically and mentally. Authorities disagreed as to the exact age that children should start. The 15th-century writer John Hardyng suggested 14 for deer hunting, but records show the young royals were well blooded by then. In the 13th century, Alexander III of Scotland was only 10 when he was given permission to hunt as he travelled through Yorkshire. Henry III agreed to his 10-year-old son Edmund of Lancaster hunting in Windsor Forest whenever he pleased. There were those who spoke out against hunting - mostly outraged that time should be wasted in such sport when people should be looking to their immortal souls.

Chivalry of games

'All young men who desire to attain ..an honorouble status.. should not concern themselves too much with nor devote too much attention to any game where greed might overcome them, such as the game of dice. One should leave playing dice for money to rakes, bawds, and tavern rogues. Yet it should be apparent that the finest games and pastimes that people who seek such honour should never tire of engaging in would be in the pastimes of jousting, conversation, dancing and singing in the company of ladies and damsels as honourably as is possible and fitting, while maintaining in word and deed and in all places their honour and status'.
The Book of Chivalry, 14th century, Geoffroi de Charny.

▼ *Portrait of a Howard boy holding a bow and arrow attributed to William Peake, 1627.* Courtesy of The Suffolk Collection, English Heritage Photographic Library

Archery

Aristocratic archery had always been associated with hunting and recreation rather than warfare. The English longbow men immortalized at the battles of Crécy and Agincourt were ordinary soldiers not nobles. As early as 1285, the Statute of Winchester required every male over 15 to possess weapons appropriate to his rank – the poorest to have at least bows and arrows. The fact that the legislation had to be later repeated suggests that it was not obeyed. In 1512 Henry VIII ordered that all male children aged between 7 and 17 should be provided with a bow and 2 arrows by the head of the household, and taught to use them. At 17 the boys were to buy or be given a bow and 4 arrows for themselves. An early example of government intervention in education with the aim of promoting universal compulsory education for boys in a particular matter.

Portrait of a 17th-century Howard boy holding a bow and arrow

The Howard family have chosen to show their un-named 5-year-old son with bow and arrow. Still in skirts (see p.14), he wears a child-sized version of the adult male doublet. His fashionable long strand of hair is known as a love-lock.

Perils of archery

Archery was not without its perils. In 13th century Bedfordshire 10-year-old John Phuch aimed his bow at the target, but hit 5-year-old Maude Boyhn. Two hundred years later in Kent 4-year-old Thomas Fowle was hit when he wandered into the range of some other child-archers. The Dean and Chapter of Exeter Cathedral complained about 'young persons' playing unsuitable games in the cloisters in 1448. One of the games mentioned was 'penny-prick' which involved shooting arrows at a penny coin.

Swords

Medieval swords were both practical fighting weapons and status symbols. In the 15th century they also began to be worn with civilian dress.

The traditional European sword of this period has a simple hilt consisting of a grip, cross-guard and pommel. The pommel balanced the weight of the blade and finished off the hilt. The grip was formed from two scales – pieces of wood or horn – sandwiching the tang or unsharpened section of the blade. An outer binding held the scales in place and gave a firm grip. The sword was used when wearing armour, so the armoured or mailed gauntlet protected the user's hand further.

These examples of children's swords all have straight double-edged blades. Their flattened diamond section makes them stronger to thrust through weak points in armour.

European sword, possibly English, about 1325

This little sword measures 80cm (31.5in) overall and is recorded as being recovered from the River Nene in Northamptonshire during dredging in the 1960s. It dates from the 14th century. Its dark colour, or patination, is typical of the effect that river water and mud have on metal. The covering of the grip has been lost, and while the damp has destroyed some of the surface of the metal, the mud has helped preserve it. Its copper alloy disc pommel bears a coat of arms, but we cannot positively identify it. IX.5501

Practice

Boys would have smaller versions of adult swords, and it is often only the size that distinguishes them. One of the military training books popular in the 12th century was the French translation from Latin of Flavius Vegetius Renatus's *Epitoma Rei Militaris*. Vegetius was a 4th-century Roman military writer, and his *Epitoma*, aimed at training Roman soldiers, was used throughout the Middle Ages as a manual for young knights. It was read in French and then English from the 15th century. Vegetius suggests that for sword practice the trainee should attack 6ft posts set into the ground using a variety of strokes. Wooden practice weapons, where used, should be heavier than normal to strengthen the student. Thrusts were preferred to cuts as they exposed less of the body to an opponent.

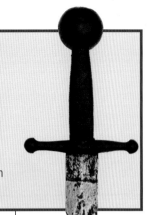

European Sword, mid 15th century

Men's swords tended to be at least a metre long, but shorter bladed weapons, more convenient for general wear and popularly known as riding swords, are found. With a blade measuring 62cm (24.75ins) this sword could be one of these, or it could be a boy's weapon. In close fighting, the heavy ball pommel could be smashed into an opponent, or the sword could be reversed, and grasped by the blade for use like a club. The grip has been replaced. The sword is one of a number recovered from the river Dordogne in France, near to the site of the battle of Castillon (1453). IX.2225

By the age of 16, a boy's training was complete. Although boys did not regularly fight in wars, there are records of teenagers in action. At 17, the future Edward II 'newly bearing arms' led a squadron of troops in his father's campaign against the Scottish castle of Caerlaverlock in 1300. His son Edward III was a youthful 14 when he commanded his first expedition against the Scots in 1327. Following in the family tradition, the Black Prince, Edward III's son, was 16 when he won his spurs at the battle of Crécy, 1346.

Boy's sword, probably English, 1475–80

It is important that objects found in the ground are carefully recorded together with details of any accompanying material. Associated objects can help us date the find, and build up a picture of when particular styles were popular. This little sword is only 62cm (24.5 in) long and was recovered from the Thames foreshore together with some coins of Edward IV (reigned 1461–83). Similar swords have survived above ground too – in churches. Here they were hung above a knight's tomb as part of his funerary achievement. IX.5427

Training for boys in full suits of armour

By the 16th century, as part of their training, boys had to get used to wearing full suits of plate armour. Armours for boys fall into three categories: for war (called 'field' armours), for foot combats (in the tournament) and for parade (ceremonial armours). Very young boys did not take part in real combat but by the age of 16 they were certainly expected to do so.

Field armour, European, end of 16th and early 17th century

This armour is for a 6-year-old boy. It is a plain armour for war training. With its full leg defences it could also have been used to practice foot combats fought against other boys within an enclosure. It weighs 7kg (16lb). II.142

Armour is not heavy

Armour is not as heavy as many people think and the weight is distributed over the whole body: a full field armour for a boy weighs about 7-18kg (16-40lb). You can move freely in armour, even doing somersaults or leaping onto your horse unaided! However, you have to get used to the articulation and overcome the problem of getting hot. There is padding underneath the steel plates and a person in armour does overheat. Boys needed to get used to the heat and the weight distribution.

Composite field half-armour, European, early 17th century

Made for a boy of about 7 years of age. This armour is made up of pieces from different armours that actually fit together very well. It shows how these boys' armours were appreciated and were used and reused by different children. The open-faced helmet would have had a padded lining to make it fit comfortably. This armour is called a half-armour as it is worn without leg-defences. II.125

Prince Henry

Shakespeare writes about young Prince Henry (the future Henry V) in his play Henry IV (part I, act IV, sc.1, l.104-110). Henry is described in full armour from head to toe, with his bevor (chin defence) and his cuisses (upper leg-defences). The Prince leaps onto his horse from the ground in full armour! This demonstrates that he is fully trained and it is a feat that could be performed by an athletic and fit young man.

I saw young Harry with his beaver on,
His cuisses on his thighs, gallantly arm'd
Rise from the ground like feather'd Mercury
And vaulted with such ease into his seat
As if an angel dropp'd down from the clouds
To turn and wind a fiery Pegasus
And witch the world with noble horsemanship.

Field armour, German, Nuremberg, about 1540
This armour is for a boy, about 16 years old, who is almost full grown. Notice the big bracket (lance-rest) on the breastplate: this youth has mastered the final skill of lance use for jousting and war. The armour weighs 19.3kg (42lb), a full adult weight. An adult armour (for his father?) was made in the same workshop in Nuremberg and is also in the Royal Armouries collection. ll.262

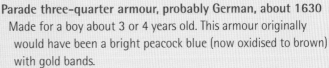

Parade three-quarter armour, probably German, about 1630
Made for a boy about 3 or 4 years old. This armour originally would have been a bright peacock blue (now oxidised to brown) with gold bands.

Some boys' armours were richly decorated, intended for the son of an emperor or king. These armours are not expensive toys intended merely for the child's amusement. Above all, they were meant to be seen and admired at important court ceremonies. At the same time they are an attempt to present the boy to spectators in his future role as military commander. Weighing 7.7kg (17lb) it would have been worn with knee-length boots. ll.163

Tournaments

Tournament armours for boys were most commonly for fighting on foot. It was useful training for boys to become accustomed to wearing armour at an early age. They would have begun to learn foot combat at about 7 years of age and to joust and tourney from 14. Aristocratic sons first practised with companions in the courts in which they grew up. Later, special contests were organised for them. One was held for young Edward I in 1256 *'so that he might be instructed in military laws'*.

Young King Henry VIII

In 1510 the young Henry VIII, aged 19, *'with two others with him challenged all comeres to fight with them at the barriers with target and casting the spear of eight feet long; and that done, his grace with the said two aides to fight every one of them twelve strokes with two-handed swords, with and against all comers, none except being a gentleman...the king behaved himself so well and delivered himself so valiently by his hardy prowess and great strength that the praise and laud was give to his grace and his aides, notwithstanding that diverse valient and strong persons had assailed him'*, Edward Hall, 16th-century chronicler.

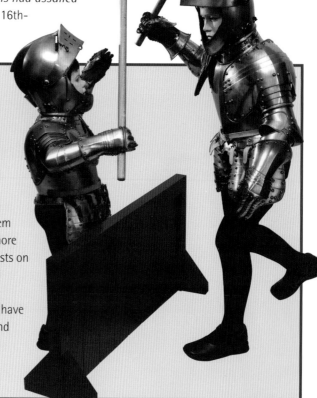

Foot-combat armours, German, probably Augsburg, about 1610

These armours were made for two brothers aged about 8 and 10 years. They may have been for the sons of Friedrich Wilhelm, Duke of Saxe-Altenburg. The two boys must have enjoyed 'practising' with each other.

There are no leg-defences because they would have fought over a barrier to keep them apart. Unlike jousting armours which have more protection on the left side and have lance-rests on the right side, these armours are completely symmetrical. The boys could give and receive blows on both sides of the body. They would have fought with blunted weapons. The armour and the clothes worn underneath would have protected against all but a little bruising perhaps. II.160, II.161

King Edward VI (1537–1553)

Edward VI became king when he was 9 years old. Like his father, Henry VIII, he was interested in sport and warfare. Court entertainments were devised not only for his amusement but also for education. When he was 10 a fake castle was built at Greenwich and this was *'besieged and assaulted to shew the king the manner of wars, wherein he had great pleasure'*. Edward learned to ride, run at the ring, shoot a bow and fight on foot with a variety of bladed weapons. He also enjoyed tennis, bowling and hunting. When he was 14 he mastered the final tournament skill of jousting.

Edward enjoyed watching tournaments and later participating in them with his team of servants and gentlemen of the court. They were fair fights and the king did not always win. Edward died in 1553 aged 15 of pneumonia, which could not be treated before the discovery of antibiotics.

Boys will be boys

Edward loved the life at court and although he took the role of kingship seriously he was still a boy. In January 1552, the boy-king had an audience with the Imperial Ambassador who wanted to discuss an important religious matter. Edward got bored and was then distracted by something amusing happening behind the ambassador. Whilst the ambassador was speaking, the boy moved to one side so that he could see 'some games' at the same time. The ambassador was not amused.

Armour made in the Royal Workshops at Greenwich under the master, Erasmus Kyrkenar, about 1550

Was this armour made for the boy-king Edward VI? It was made in the Royal Workshops which were founded by Henry VIII. At this time the Royal Workshop only made armours by order of the King. Here is a royal armour made for a boy of about 12 years old when a boy of about that age was King of England. Despite the mystery that this royal armour was found in Cotehele House, Cornwall, in 1956 and was not part of the indigenous collection which passed into the Tower of London, it is assuredly that of the young king.

This is a light cavalry armour with an unusual articulated cuirass that is very flexible. The helmet and gauntlets are missing. In April 1551 Edward VI *'mounted his horse in full armour, rode two or three miles each time, and also charged the target to exercise and show himself to the people'.* II.178

In the picture

Sadly we have no examples of Tudor children's weapons in the collection, but there is plenty of pictorial evidence from the period.

Having your portrait painted was a major family event in Tudor times. Only the richest could afford it, and they lost no opportunity to impress the onlooker. Dress was best, carefully selected to show wealth and status. Children were included. While Tudor sons were still in the nursery they wore skirts like their sisters. Boys entered the adult world when they were 'breeched', usually between the ages of 5-7. They would wear adult male style dress on formal occasions

▼ *Portrait of King Henry VIII, after Hans Holbein the Younger, about 1545.* Board of Trustees of the National Museums and Galleries on Merseyside

▶ *Portrait of King Edward VI, aged 9, unknown artist, about 1547.* National Portrait Gallery

▼ *The Sidney family in 1596.* Reproduced by kind permission of Viscount De L'Isle, from his private collection at Penshurst Place.

Like father, like son

The court of Edward VI was like that of Henry VIII. Like Henry in his youth Edward enjoyed the martial pursuits proper to his status, and courtiers, recognizing this presented him with suitable gifts such as falcons and greyhounds. Few gifts more obviously pleased the king than the 12 horses and 2 mules sent by King Henri II of France. Edward recorded his gifts in his diary which has survived. It was started under supervision of his tutors but became his own personal account and it is the masques and jousts that are recorded with relish rather than the sermons.

The Sidney family

In group portraits, swords are often the only way to tell the younger boys from the girls. Here a skirted Master William Sidney, surrounded by his siblings, carries a fine feathered bonnet and rests his hand on his rapier. Originally developed on the continent, the rapier swept through the fashionable courts of Europe and England. Essentially a thrusting weapon, it was regarded with suspicion by traditionalists who resented its popularity and bemoaned its effectiveness. All too often its long blade proved fatal, and a whole new school of swordplay and fencing masters arose round it.

William did not live long enough to prove his swordsmanship. Infant and child mortality was high. Younger brother Robert – shown here with coral teether and dressed in the cap and apron of the very young – survived to inherit the title.

Darling Darnley

Nine-year-old Henry Stuart regards the world with confidence. The eldest surviving son of Matthew Stuart, Earl of Lennox, and Lady Margaret Douglas, he was the great grandson of Henry VII through his mother's family. Fashionably dressed, he sports a sword and dagger. Sword hilts had become more complicated. Increasing civilian use meant that no armoured gauntlets were worn, yet changes in fighting techniques required more protection for the swordsman. Additional bars, known as guards, wove around the grip and cross-guard to enclose and defend the hand. The sword and left-hand dagger were a popular fighting combination. They also afforded the wearer a further opportunity to display his wealth by the richness of their decoration.

◄ Portrait of Henry Stuart, Lord Darnley (1545-1567) attributed to Hans Eworth. Scottish National Portrait Gallery

▼ Portrait of Henry Stuart, Lord Darnley, and Charles Stuart (later Earl of Lennox), 1562, attributed to Hans Eworth. The Royal Collection © 2003, Her Majesty Queen Elizabeth II

Brothers in arms

Eight years later, Henry Stuart is shown with his younger brother Charles. Their mother hoped to further the family fortunes by marrying Henry to the recently widowed Mary Queen of Scots, three years his senior. The original portrait was painted on fabric – convenient to roll up and take to his prospective bride. In 1565 they were married. Their son the future James I of England and VI of Scotland was born in June 1566 . Unfortunately it was not a match made in heaven, and in 1567 Darnley's lodgings were blown up. He was found dead nearby, apparently untouched by the explosion. Darnley was only 22.

Brother Charles fared little better. He became Earl of Lennox and married Elizabeth Cavendish. Their daughter, Arabella Stuart (1575–1615) spent the last years of her life in the Tower having married against her cousin James's wishes. Charles died from consumption aged 20 in 1576.

In the portrait Henry rests his hand on his sword hilt, neatly demonstrating the limitations of paintings in identifying swords. The main dating feature of a sword is its hilt, and all too often a careless hand obscures the finer details. Charles, still in skirts (aged 8 wearing a scholar's gown, rather than nurserywear) has a dagger hilt peeping out from under his right arm. Shakespeare gave Leontes, the King of Sicilia in *The Winter's Tale* these wistful lines in Act I Scene II:

..I did recoil
Twenty-three years, and saw myself unbreech'd,
In my green velvet coat, my dagger muzzled,
Lest it bite its master, and so prove,
As ornaments oft do, too dangerous

Henry, Prince of Wales (1594 – 1612)

Prince Henry was the eldest son of James I and heir to the throne. England and Scotland became one united kingdom when James VI of Scotland became James I of England. The House of Stuart had begun.

In a letter of 31 October 1606 de la Boderie, the French ambassador, writes of the Prince, aged 12:

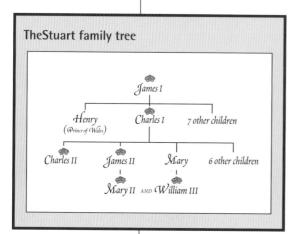

TheStuart family tree

- James I
  - Henry (Prince of Wales)
  - Charles I
    - Charles II
    - James II
      - Mary II AND William III
    - Mary
    - 6 other children
  - 7 other children

'He is a particular lover of horses and what belongs to them, but is not fond of hunting; and when he goes to it it is rather for the pleasure of galloping than that which the dogs give him. He plays willingly enough at tennis, and at another Scots diversion very like mall [probably golf]; but this always with persons older than himself, as if he despised those of his own age. He studies two hours, and employs the rest of his time in tossing the pike, or leaping, or shooting with the bow, or throwing the bar, or vaulting, or some other exercise of that kind; and he is never idle!'

The prince was much fonder of outdoor sport than of study and was very keen on tournaments and the arts of warfare.

On 10 October 1612, when he was 18 years old, he became severely ill but ignored the symptoms. He even went out and played tennis in chilly weather. He died shortly after of typhoid fever.

The young prince was also very well behaved and even installed swear-boxes. He ordered boxes at his several houses, *'causing all those who did swear in his hearing to pay money to the same, which were after duly given to the poor'.*

Sabatons, English, Greenwich about 1610
This pair of foot-defences are called sabatons. Strangely, they are all that remain of a missing armour. They were made in the English royal workshops which had been founded by Henry VIII almost a hundred years earlier. They show the great skills of the Master Armourer William Pickering. All the steel plates have been riveted together in such a way as to allow the foot to bend fully. III.4625

Portrait of Henry, Knight of the Garter

This portrait was painted when Henry was 10 years old and his father, James I, had recently been crowned King of England. Henry has just been made a knight of the chivalrous Order of the Garter and is shown wearing the robes. At the ceremony he had impressed the courtiers with his *'quick, witty answers, princely carriage, and reverend obeisance at the altar.'*

   Because of the spread of the plague, when this portrait was painted, the prince had just moved from Windsor to Oatlands, Surrey, where he set up his own household, complete with servants and retainers.

Portrait of Henry, Prince of Wales in the hunting field

This may be a commemorative portrait of 16-year-old Henry as Prince of Wales. He is shown with his sword drawn in an heroic pose and with his hunting companions. He and his horse look out of the picture at the spectator.

▲ *Portrait of Henry, Knight of the Garter by Robert Peake, 1604*, in the collection of the Earl of Mar and Kellie.

◄ *Attributed to Robert Peake, about 1610.* The Royal Collection © 2003, Her Majesty Queen Elizabeth II

Armour, Dutch, about 1609

This armour was a gift given by Sir Francis Vere to Henry, Prince of Wales, in 1609. Henry was about 15 years old at the time. He was already strongly interested in military matters. The following year he was presented at court in a chivalrous spectacle written by Ben Johnson, in which he fought as chief challenger. Later that year he was made Prince of Wales.

The surfaces have an astonishing etched and gilt decoration. Heroic fighting warriors can be seen all over the armour. This wonderful decoration has scenes taken from one of the ancient Roman biographies of the life of Alexander the Great. This book was still given to boys in the 17th century as a model to follow. As Henry was not fond of study, perhaps his tutors thought it was a way of getting him to learn his lessons! II.88.

Portrait of Henry, Prince of Wales

This is a symbolic picture with hidden meanings. Henry, Prince of Wales is shown here as bringing the chivalry of King Arthur back to England. The clues to this are the Arthurian themes embroidered on his skirts and saddle cloth. The naked figure is Father Time who carries the Prince's lance and helmet. Time is tied by the forelock to Henry. He brings opportunity for a brilliant future for the future King of England. Henry died of typhoid fever two years later.

▲ *Portrait of Henry, Prince of Wales by Robert Peake, about 1610.* From the collection at Parham Park, West Sussex.

Parts of an armour, English, Greenwich, about 1603

Was this armour made for the 9-year-old Henry, Prince of Wales or another prince or aristocrat? This wonderfully crafted helmet and cuirass were made in the Royal Workshops in Greenwich and were part of a complete armour, the remainder of which is, sadly, now lost.

The breastplate is most unusual, since it has two holes for the attachment of a lance-rest. This is astonishing as it means that the armour was used for cavalry training with a lance (jousting) which did not normally begin until 14 years of age. There is a long horizontal slit in the helmet for vision and below that many vertical slits for breathing. Portraits painted during the 17th century often show helmets like this armet set down on a convenient table. They are nearly always shown with the visor raised. II.124

Charles I (1600 – 1649)

Charles was the younger brother of Henry, Prince of Wales, and was a very sickly child who was not expected to survive. At the age of 3 he still could not walk or speak properly. Although he became a good horseman and walker, he suffered from a speech impediment all his life. He had to learn to speak carefully and slowly and was a serious child.

▲ *Portrait of Charles when Duke of York by Robert Peake, 1605.* Bristol City Museum and Art Gallery/Bridgeman Art Library

Portrait of Charles when Duke of York

Charles is 5 years old in this painting. He is so young that he is still in skirts. One hand is on his sword and the other holds a ceremonial staff. Beside him on a table are parts of an armour: the helmet and gauntlets. The collar of the armour is around his neck.

A few days after his 5th birthday, in a dazzling suit and gleaming with jewels, he was taken to court, carried by lords and attendants into the Palace of Whitehall. Here he was created Duke of York and, at a great feast in the Banqueting Hall, he sat at the head of a special table in his high chair.

For most of his early childhood Prince Charles led a quiet country life, moving from one of the royal palaces to another in the care of Lady Cary and his tutors.

He was devoted to his brilliant elder brother Henry. In one of his letters he wrote: *'Sweet, sweet brother, I will give anything that I have to you: both my horse and my books and my pieces and my cross-bows or anything that you would have. Good brother, love me and I shall ever love and serve you.'* In another letter he urged his brother to come and visit, *'for to enjoy your company, to ride with you, to hunt with you, will give me the greatest of pleasure.'*

This was written in Latin (perhaps with help from his tutor) when Charles was only 8 years old.

Brotherly love!

As with all brothers, the two princes did squabble. One day, the boys were in a room next door to one in which their father was consulting the Archbishop of Canterbury. His Grace's hat lay on a table. Henry picked it up and, teasing Charles for his seriousness and learning, placed it on his brother's head with the promise that when he was king he would make him a pious archbishop. Charles, crossly threw it to the ground and trampled it underfoot.

Despite being small, Charles became a good sportsman. He could ride well and took part in jousts as well as being an excellent shot. He was also accomplished at golf and tennis which he played from the age of 10. He became Prince of Wales at his brother's death and later king. He was beheaded in 1649.

Armour, probably English, about 1630

This tiny armour is only 95cm (37.5 in) tall. There have been many questions about its ownership. In the 18th century it was thought to have belonged to Richard, Duke of York, one of the princes supposedly murdered in the Tower in about 1485. In the 19th century it was suggested that it was made for Jeffrey Hudson, the court dwarf of Henrietta Maria, queen of Charles I. It was at least dated correctly, but Jeffrey Hudson was only 46cm (18 in) tall at the time.

Finally, the mystery was solved when it was noticed that Charles I was shown wearing the helmet in a sculpted portrait at Stourhead House. The distinctive dragon crest is unique and could not be mistaken.

There are still further questions that have not been answered. Did it belong to Charles himself as a small child? It seems too small for any child to wear, particularly with its narrow arm-defences. Charles, however, was an extremely sickly child who suffered from rickets and could still barely walk at the age of 7. He had small limbs and grew no taller than 163cm (5ft 4 in).

It is perhaps most likely that it was an armourer's demonstration piece for an armour that was never made or that has been lost. Clearly, Charles kept it and liked it enough to have his portrait sculpted wearing the helmet as an adult. ll.126

▲ *Bronze bust of King Charles I by Hubert Le Sueur.* Stourhead House, Wiltshire. NTPL/John Bethell

One armour, three kings – one armour passed to 3 generations of kings

Armour of Charles I and also Charles II, Dutch, about 1615

This horseman's armour was made for Charles I when he was about 15 years old, possibly when he became Prince of Wales. It later passed to his son Charles II and then to his grandson William III. It weighs 19.5 kg (43 lb) which is a normal weight for an adult armour.

This armour is stylishly and lavishly decorated with narrow gold bands ornamented with scrolling foliage. The pattern was made with an engraving tool and punches. The steel plates of the saddle and even the horses' head defence (shaffron) are decorated to match.

This armour has more special features. It has extra pieces that allow it to be used for fighting on foot. By wearing the cuirass (breastplate) and adding a light open helmet (it looks like a hat), short thigh defences (tassets) and a large round shield, the armour could be used when dismounted. II.90

Portrait of Charles II

Young Prince Charles, son of Charles I, aged about 14, is shown wearing the armour and a sword. One hand rests on his helmet and the other holds a baton of command. He had just been made the commander of a troop of Lifeguards formed of northern noblemen and gentlemen who had offered their services to the king.

▶ *Portrait of Charles II by William Dobson, about 1644.* The Royal Collection © 2003, Her Majesty Queen Elizabeth II

▼ *Portrait of William as Duke of Orange, Dutch, about 1677.* I.40

Portrait of King William III as Duke of Orange

William was the grandson of Charles I and nephew of Charles II. He grew up in Holland and had an active military career. Aged 26, he was hit in the arm by a musket ball at the siege of Maestricht in 1676.

The following year he came to England to marry Princess Mary, the daughter of James II. It is possible that this is when he was painted in his uncle's armour. Since the armour is only 145 cm (4 ft 9 in) tall the adult William could not have worn it, so the artist has adjusted its size in this painting. I.40

Charles II (1630 – 1685)

Charles was the first child to be born heir to all 3 kingdoms. He was a dark-haired and vivacious child. He grew up in a happy family – his French mother bore a total of 9 children in 14 years. The children spent their winters at St James's Palace in London and their summers touring various country palaces such as Greenwich, Hampton Court, Oatlands and Richmond.

Letter from Prince Charles to his tutor, Lord Newcastle

My Lord, I would not have you take too much physick: for it doth allwaies make me worse, and I think it will do the like with you. I ride every day, and am ready to follow any other directions from you. Make hast to returne to him that loves you. Charles P

Portrait of Charles in armour

Charles, aged 8, is dressed in a full cuirassier armour with his hand on his plumed helmet and holding a pistol. Cuirassier armour was worn with boots and it was the last time full cavalry armour was worn on the battlefield.

▲ *Portrait of Charles II in armour by Anthony Van Dyck, 1638.* National Portrait Gallery

Harquebusier armour, English, Greenwich, about 1638-40

The helmet of this armour demonstrates that the young prince Charles was given the latest in technology and fashion. This is one of the earliest examples of a characteristic English harquebusier helmet with its distinctive triple-barred face guard. The harquebusier was a light cavalryman who was to supercede the cuirassier or heavy cavalryman.

The armour appears bright and shiny as though highly polished, but this is due to to fact that it is actually silvered all over. It was also originally gilt but only small traces of the gold have survived. Panels of decoration are filled with trophies of armour, weapons, banners and musical instruments. All the decoration is punched and engraved. On the collar (gorget) the trophies are embossed in relief.

The breastplate has a mysterious secret. The pointed shape would date it to about 1610. But Prince Charles was born in 1630. On looking closely inside, it is possible to see distinct lines laying out the decoration for a larger breastplate, clearly left unfinished and later used to tailor this piece for Charles. The decoration of the first breastplate used thistles which pointed to another prince: Henry, Prince of Wales who was Charles' uncle. An armour of Henry in the Royal Collection, at Windsor Castle has this design of thistles on it. II.92

▲ *Portrait of Charles II wearing the Charles I armour by William Dobson, 1643.*
Scottish National Portrait Gallery

Portrait of Charles II wearing the Charles I armour

Charles is 13 in this portrait and is shown in a military pose dressed in his breastplate over his military buff-coat and holding his baton of command. His page is holding his helmet. He is wearing his father's armour (II.90, see page 22)

I fear them not

In 1642 Charles, aged 12, and his 9-year-old brother James saw their first battle. According to a contemporary account, the Princes were taken to Edgehill by their tutor and physician, Dr William Harvey, who sat down under a hedge to read a book. Only when a cannon ball hit the ground nearby did he hastily move the young princes. They narrowly escaped being captured by Parliamentarian troops. Charles pulled out his pistol and shouting '*I fear them not*' prepared to charge. Fortunately, they were saved from this rash action by the arrival of a Royalist captain.

Charles stayed with his father during the early stages of the English Civil War until he was laid low by an attack of measles. He escaped to France when he was 16. He succeeded his father as king of Great Britain in name only in 1649 while he was in exile and Cromwell ruled England as Lord Protector. He was officially crowned king in Westminster Abbey in 1661. He died in 1685 from a stroke.

Small bronze cannon, English, 1638 by John Browne

This little bronze cannon is one of a set of 10 made for the 8-year-old Prince of Wales, later Charles II. His badge of 3 ostrich feathers appears on the barrel of the gun and the side, or cheek, of its wooden carriage. The founder's name, John Browne, is included on the cannon. Browne made 5 and Thomas Pitt a further 5 in 1639.

After Charles I's execution in 1649, a sale catalogue of the Royal property was made, and these cannon appear in lot 28 with a number of military models. By 1665 they are listed among the curiosities in the Tower. Their original carriages were destroyed in the Grand Storehouse Fire of 1841, and replaced by new ones in 1849. XIX.24

James II (1633 – 1701)

James, born in 1633, was the younger brother of Charles II and unlike him was fair-haired and calm by nature.

He had followed his father Charles I during the Civil War but was left behind in Oxford. He was imprisoned for some time finally escaping under cover of a game of hide-and-seek in 1648. James was then taken to the river Thames near London Bridge and escaped to the continent, disguised in women's clothes. He settled at the Hague with his sister, the Princess of Orange, but later joined his mother and brother Charles in France.

As an adult he had a distinguished military career. He succeeded his brother as King James II when he was 51. James abdicated in 1688 by fleeing to France and died of a stroke in 1701. His daughter became Mary II.

Portrait of James, Duke of York and Charles I

This is one of the last portraits of James with his father. It was painted in 1647 when James was 14.

▼ *Portrait of James, Duke of York and Charles I by Peter Lely, 1647.* Scottish National Portrait Gallery

Sir Walter Raleigh (1552 – 1618)

Sir Walter Raleigh was born in Devon in about 1552. He was an adventurer who had fought in France and Ireland, and sailed against the Spanish seeking gold and land. In 1581 he attracted Elizabeth I's attention and reaped the rewards of her favour. In 1593 he was detained in the Tower at the Queen's displeasure, having secretly married one of her ladies in waiting, Bess Throckmorton. On his release he 'retired' to his country estates.

Portrait of Sir Walter Raleigh and his son Wat

▼ *Portrait of Sir Walter Raleigh and his son Wat, anon, 1602.* National Portrait Gallery

In this portrait of 1602, the Walter Raleighs have every reason to look forward to a successful future. Although Sir Walter had enjoyed military success – he was the admiral in command of the triumphant expedition against the Spanish at Cadiz in 1596 – he has chosen to be shown in civilian dress. Young Wat, at 9, sports the Elizabethan equivalent of 'designer' clothing. He favours the falling band collar over his father's more traditional ruff, and longer breeches. As gentlemen, father and son both wear swords, but Wat does not appear to have a matching dagger.

Elizabeth's successor James disliked Raleigh and stripped him of many of the estates and offices he held. Falsely accused of conspiring against the new king, Raleigh was sentenced to death, commuted at the last minute to life imprisonment in the Tower.

Walter turned his attention to science and writing. His friendship with James's eldest son, Prince Henry inspired him to write *The History of the World* – designed to broaden the prince's education. With Henry's sudden death in 1612, the project went no further than the first volume (published in 1614), and Raleigh's hope of release faded. In 1616 he persuaded James to let him mount an expedition to find gold in South America. It was a doomed venture, and Wat died accompanying his father. Raleigh returned to England, and execution in 1618.

Firearms

The 17th century saw growth in the availability and use of firearms. Aged 8 the future Charles II carries a pistol with his armour in Van Dyk's portrait of him (see p.23). Thirty years later, the young James Cecil at 2 is too young for armour but has a pistol at his feet. It is unclear whether this is a toy, or indicates a future military career. His sister, a sophisticated 5, has graduated to adult style gowns, albeit with leading strings – the ribbon-like strips hanging from her shoulders.

As an adult, James enthusiastically, but unsuccessfully supported his namesake King James II. When the king was deposed in 1688, James was imprisoned in the Tower of London. On his release, he retired to the family home in Hatfield, Hertfordshire, dying in 1694.

◄ *James Cecil, 4th Earl of Salisbury (1666 – 94), and his eldest sister, Lady Catherine Cecil, later Lady Downing (1663 – 88) by John Michael Wright, about 1668.*
By courtesy of the Marquess of Salisbury.

'The grand distinguishing mark of a gentleman is the wearing of a sword' stated *Connoisseur* magazine in 1754.

In the early 18th century boys would be breeched on formal occasions as young as 3 and 4 years old. They would also wear a sword, and sometimes carry a cane too. For the very young, the advantage of the sword over a cane was that it could be wedged in its scabbard and firmly tied to the wearer, thereby lessening its destructive potential. There were no such possibilities with a cane.

Garton Orme

It might seem overkill to wear your sword while playing a musical instrument, but young Master Orme is not alone in doing this. Thomas Arne is shown conducting an orchestra in 1770 complete with sword. In this picture the sword and spinet are both accessories – demonstrating Garton's status and talents.

▶ Garton Orme at the spinet by Thomas Hill, 1704/5. Holburne Museum of Art, Bath

▼ Portrait of Prince Charles Edward Stuart (1720 –1788) by Louis Gabriel Blanchet, 1738. National Portrait Gallery

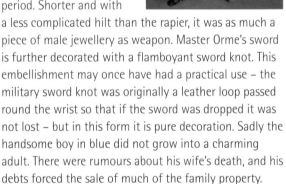

The small-sword had become the preferred civilian dress sword of the period. Shorter and with a less complicated hilt than the rapier, it was as much a piece of male jewellery as weapon. Master Orme's sword is further decorated with a flamboyant sword knot. This embellishment may once have had a practical use – the military sword knot was originally a leather loop passed round the wrist so that if the sword was dropped it was not lost – but in this form it is pure decoration. Sadly the handsome boy in blue did not grow into a charming adult. There were rumours about his wife's death, and his debts forced the sale of much of the family property.

Portrait of Bonnie Prince Charlie, Prince Charles Edward Stuart (1720 – 1788)

Armour continued to play a part in formal portraits. Here Bonnie Prince Charlie, the Young Pretender stakes his claim to the British throne. He is wearing a breastplate and backplate, and rests his arm on a plumed helmet. The armour is little more than a decorative prop, but affords him some military gravitas.

The grandson of James II, he grew up in exile. His attempts to regain the English throne ended at Culloden in 1746, and he fled abroad.

Sir James MacDonald (1741–1766) and Sir Alexander MacDonald (c.1745–1795)

By the middle of the century, children were beginning to be portrayed less formally. The brothers MacDonald are shown at play. Young Alexander, in tartan trews, practises his golf swing under the watchful eye of his older brother James. Master James lounges with his sporting gun. The defeat of the Jacobites and Bonnie Prince Charlie in 1746 had led to a ban on the wearing of tartan in civilian dress, but the MacDonalds have chosen to ignore this. This may be a bold political statement, or may indicate that they are confident enough of their position not to worry.

Although swords were being laid aside from all but the most formal civilian dress by the end of the century, they were still seen in the military context.

Captain William Congreve (1741 – 1814) and his son William (1772 – 1828)

The William Congreves both pursued successful artillery careers, and both were Comptrollers of the Royal Laboratory at Woolwich. In 1808, young William invented a rocket for use in war. A copy of the painting is prominently displayed at the family home. The rest of the family are shown in domestic harmony - brother Thomas playing with a toy artillery piece while his sister shows off her pet squirrel!

▲ *Portrait of Sir James MacDonald (1741-1766) and Sir Alexander MacDonald (c.1745-1795) attributed to William Mosman, c. late 1740s.*
Scottish National Portrait Gallery

◄ *Portrait of Captain William Congreve (1741 – 1814) and his son William (1772 - 1828) by Philip Reinagle, 1782.*
National Gallery of Ireland

◄ *Portrait of Mrs Congreve with her children by Philip Reinagle, 1782.*
National Gallery of Ireland

The boys' small-swords in the Royal Armouries' collection are distinguished from their grown-up counterparts only by their size. They are perfect miniatures of the adult model.

France was the style capital of Europe, setting the fashions of the day. In England pattern books of the latest decorative designs and motifs were produced and circulated round the country. Of course it took time for the new trends to become established, and there was often a significant delay before the provinces followed the fashions of the capital.

French small-sword, Paris, hilt with Parisian hallmarks for 1722–27

This Parisian small-sword has an exquisite silver hilt covered with a gold wash. The decoration includes scrolls and shells – fashionable motifs that spread from France throughout Europe. Taking its name from the French *rocaille* or rockwork, rococo decoration was applied to everything from furniture to weapons. The tapering triangular-section blade is far from frivolous. IX.1842

English small-sword, early 18th century,

Traditional motifs remained popular. This sword has a hilt alive with charging horsemen, while an armoured figure lounges on the knuckle-guard.

The sword comes from the collection of Sir Andrew Fountaine (1676–1753) of Narford Hall, Norfolk. A famous collector, Sir Andrew presumably acquired this miniature sword as a curiosity. In his day job, Sir Andrew succeeded Sir Isaac Newton as Warden of the Mint in the Tower in 1727. IX.2128

Youth's small-sword, possibly English, blade German

Small-swords were made for bigger boys too. The sword pictured is almost adult sized. It is fitted with a German blade considered at the time among the best. It is a reminder of the serious side of swords – however beautiful the hilt, these are still deadly weapons. It has a slim triangular-section blade and it requires serious study to master the art of its use. A gentleman never knew when he might be called on to defend his honour in a duel. The blade is inscribed *Quis separet nos nil nisi mors?*– what shall separate us except death? IX.799

Boy's small-sword, hilt English, blade French, about 1775

Not all small-swords had a shell-guard. Loop-guards were also fashionable. Based on military patterns of the time, they had an outer bar connecting the root of the knuckle-guard and the rear quillon. This example has a hilt made from facetted steel. This was a popular alternative to precious metal for hilts, and was a fashion pioneered in England. Modern court and civil swords continue to use similar hilts. The blade is French. Unusually its scabbard and part of its sword belt have survived – all too often they are lost. It is said to have belonged to Prince Octavius, George III's 8th son and 13th child. Born in February 1779, he died in May 1783. If indeed he did wear this sword it would have been with formal court dress. IX.2171A

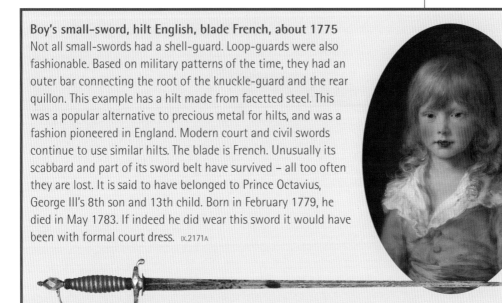

▲ *Prince Octavius by Thomas Gainsborough (1727–88)*. The Royal Collection © 2003, Her Majesty Queen Elizabeth II

Small-sword, early 18th century

In contrast this sword is only 42cms (16.5ins) long, but is perfectly proportioned for a very young boy – perhaps his first dress sword, and very much for best. It is comparatively plain, and may appear more attractive to the modern eye than some of its gaudier relatives. Its silver hilt is unmarked, so there are no clues to its date or place of manufacture. Similar hilts were found throughout Europe, but the English do seem to have been particularly fond of these understated silver hilts. IX.2553

No self-respecting Georgian gentleman would have been without his sporting guns. Highly decorated guns shoot no further or more accurately than their plainer cousins, but they do catch the eye.

To be a good shot requires much practice, and scaled-down guns were produced for children to learn with. They are usually identified by their size, more specifically the distance from the trigger to the butt, known as the 'draw'. All the children's guns we have from this period are muzzle-loaders, i.e. the charge had to be put down the barrel and rammed home to ensure it was in the correct position. After the gun had been fired, the barrel would have to be cleaned out and the loading procedure repeated.

Child's sporting gun, German, about 1720
This little gun has been much altered - presumably as new generations of the family came to use it. Originally fitted with a flintlock mechanism it has been modernised, in the early 19th century, by the substitution of a percussion lock. The barrel has been shortened. XII.330

Flintlock sporting gun, English, about 1720, by David Wynn
Included in the decoration of this gun is an Earl's coronet above the letter 'D'. It is believed to have belonged to William Cochrane, 5th Earl of Dundonald. He inherited the title in 1720, aged 12, and died 4 years later. David Wynn worked in London as a gunsmith from 1715 until 1729. XII.5222

Boy's flintlock sporting gun, German, dated 1723

Highly decorated sporting guns were made for children, especially princes. Sebastian Hauschka, gunmaker to the Duke of Brunswick, made this fine flintlock sporting gun for the 13-year-old Louis XV of France (1710–1774). The inlaid silver decoration combines sporting motifs (boars, stags and dogs), the French coat of arms and Louis' monogram.

XII.4855

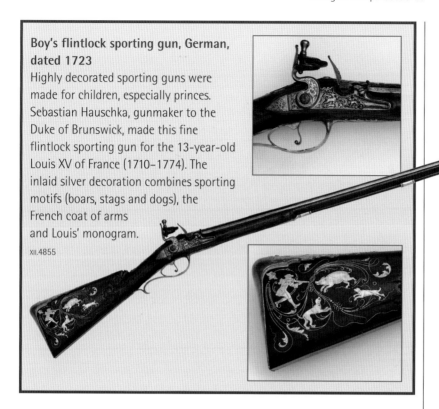

Child's stonebow, German or English, late 18th century

Crossbows had long been used for hunting – Archduke Maximilian is shown with one in the 15th century (see p.39). By the 18th century stonebows were a popular alternative to guns for hunting small game, especially birds. Named after the small pellets they shot (usually made from stone, but lead or baked clay were also used), they could be very accurate at close range.

This child-sized model is incomplete. The damage suggests that it has been well, if carelessly, used. XI.110

By the end of the 18th century the sword had been dropped from general wear, but it remained part of formal court dress and military uniform. Throughout the 19th and into the 20th century, the cavalry continued to use their swords in anger. On the continent there was a fashion for soldiers' sons to wear miniature versions of their fathers' uniforms complete with swords.

Shooting remained a gentlemanly leisure pursuit, and so children's guns continued to be custom made for the sons of the landed gentry and the more upwardly mobile middle classes.

Boy's court sword and scabbard, English, London, about 1900
This sword is a puzzle. It was bought as being of the type that might be carried by pages at court. With its simple cross-hilt, horse head pommel and dog's head ends to the quillons, it is not a fighting sword. The sword knot dangling from the pommel is modelled on military patterns of the later 19th century, but could have joined the sword later. Unfortunately it does not conform to any published regulation patterns of court sword we have found. IX.2158

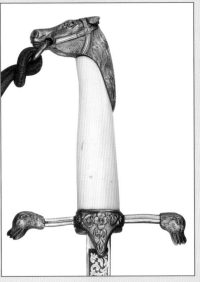

Boy's military style sword, French, early 19th century

This little sword dates from the Napoleonic Empire. It sports a fashionable stirrup hilt (so called because of its shape) and its curved blade bears the inscription in gilt letters *Garde Imperiale/du Roi de Rome*. Napolcon's infant son François was created King of Rome in 1811, and a guard named in his honour. At only 61cms (24ins) long, this sword was probably intended as a costume accessory for an officer's son.

The French philosopher Jean Jacques Rousseau (1712–1778) had condemned the French 'hussar' fashion of dressing little boys in military style clothing. He favoured less restrictive styles of dress, and a freer, more child-friendly approach to childhood and education. His ideas were not always new, but his writings were widely read, and influential. Sadly this advocate of child liberation found it impossible to both write and support his children. Five of the junior Rousseaus found themselves growing up in Paris foundling hospitals, although their father sought to justify his actions in later life. ıx.1095

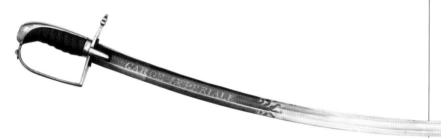

Boy's sabre and scabbard, French, about 1820

The fashion for mini-military wear continued. This is a scaled-down version of the French cavalry sword of the early 19th century. Side-guards linking the knuckle-guard and rear-quillon give additional protection to the hand. The curved blade was intended to cut rather than thrust. The nicks along the cutting edge suggest that someone couldn't resist trying it out. ıx.1250

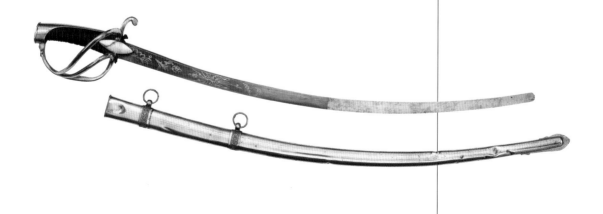

HRH Prince George of Cambridge

Britain's links with the German states were strong under the Hanoverian kings – it was only when Victoria became Queen that the title Elector of Hanover was given up (girls couldn't be Electors). George William Frederick Charles was born on 26 March 1819 in Hanover where his father was Governor General. He was the grandchild of George III, and was briefly first in line to the British throne until his cousin Victoria's arrival later the same year.

Boy soldier

At the age of 9 George became a colonel in the Jäger Battalion of the Hanover Guard. From 1830 George lived at the British Court under the care of his uncle William IV, returning to Hanover in 1836.

For Queen and Country

In 1837, with Victoria's accession, the Cambridges returned to England. George began his military career which was to last for 58 years. He was stationed in Leeds in the summer of 1842, peace-keeping in an industrial dispute. He served in the Crimean War (1854–56) with some distinction, but was invalided home.

George became General Commanding in Chief of the British Army in 1856. The 19th century was a time of sweeping reforms in the structure and equipment of the British Army. As a conservative career soldier, George often found himself personally opposed to the changes, but he was recognized by his contemporaries as hard working and with the best interests of the army at heart. Above all he was seen as fair.

Retirement!

He was finally persuaded to retire, reluctantly, in 1895. However he continued to play a part in official life. A sprightly 78 he insisted on riding in Victoria's Diamond Jubilee Procession of 1897. Four years later he was again on horseback, this time at her funeral. He died in March 1904, just short of his 85th birthday, and is buried next to his beloved wife Louisa in Kensal Green Cemetery, London.

Stand of 5 flintlock muskets made for George Duke of Cambridge, about 1830

This stand of 5 muskets was made in Germany, probably by Crause at the Herzberg Arms Factory for George when he was about 10 or 11 years old. Four of them (XII.1775-8) are boy-sized versions of the India Pattern musket, one of the British infantryman's standard longarms of the Napoleonic Wars (1800–15). Even though they were muzzle-loaders, in trained hands they could produce a formidable rate of fire.

The fifth (XII. 1779) was made in Belgium, and of poorer quality than the others. Fitted with a French style bayonet which has been blunted, it probably appeared a better match when it was new. XII.1775–9

Boy's centre-fire 24-bore sporting gun, French, Paris, by Gastinne Renette

This perfectly proportioned child's sporting gun was produced by the French gunmaker Gastinne Renette. Its neo-Gothic style of decoration became popular after the Great Exhibition of 1851. Running from 1 May to 15 October the Great Exhibition owed much to the enthusiasm of Victoria's husband Prince Albert. Housed in the specially constructed Crystal Palace in Hyde Park, it was intended to showcase the best in modern design and practice. Hugely popular, it spawned other similar, smaller scale events. This gun may indeed be an exhibition piece. It was recently purchased by the Armouries as a fine example of the gunmaker's craft as well as adding to our children's collection. XII.11307

Boyz toyz

▼ Children's Games *by Peter Breughel the Elder, 1560.* Kunthistorisches Museum/ Bridgeman Art Library

Not all children's weapons were intended for serious use. Children have always played, and its importance in their development has been long recognised.

Toys are found from earliest times, often made in imitation of objects from the adult world.

Wooden swords

In the late 18th century the Yeomanry Volunteers of Alnwick, Northumberland, had wooden bladed swords to practice with. From early times younger boys would also have practised with wooden swords to accustom them to the weight of the real thing before serious training began. Safer for young fighters than their metal counterparts, they could be easily replaced when broken.

Toy lances

Illustrations of children playing with toy lances exist, they often have windmill-like sails on the tips. In Breughel's painting of children playing, if you look carefully you can see two youthful jousters. It is difficult to tell if they are boys or girls. The painting shows over 200 children playing more than 80 different games, many of which are familiar to us today. Of course some parents could afford to buy their children custom-made toys, often with a built-in educational value – but this was beyond the means of most.

Archduke Maximilian (1459–1519) at play

Maximilian, wearing a coronet, is shown learning various skills. Like Charles II (p.24) he has a toy cannon and is lighting the priming at the touch-hole to fire it. Elsewhere he aims a crossbow and strings his longbow. To the right of the picture a rather grand arena has been set up, and he is playing with model knights against another boy. Maximilian's knight has struck home with his lance, and his opponent's knight falls back. The young Archduke grew up to become the Holy Roman Emperor Maximilian I (1493–1519) in what is modern Germany and Austria, and he was famous for his jousting skills.

◄ *From* Der Weisskunig, (The White King) – *a 15th-century illustrated autobiography of Maximilian I.*

Toy guns

Small cast brass guns like those shown below, usually no more than 15cms (6 ins) long, have turned up on archaeological sites all round the country from Yorkshire to Wiltshire. Most come from the London area. They first appear in the Elizabethan period and continued to be made into the 17th century. We are not sure which end of the market they were aimed at – little men or big boys – but we know that they worked. Some have been found with their barrels burst through overloading with gunpowder.

Perhaps these guns made for the job were safer than homemade ones. Richard Carew , the Cornish topographer, records how the boys of Bodmin school in 1548 divided into factions representing the old religion and the new. One of the more adventurous lads *'converted the spill* [stem] *of an old candlestick to a gun, charged it with powder and a stone, and (through mischance or ungraciousness) therewith killed a calf, whereupon the owner complained, the master whipped, and the division ended'.*

Toy pistol, English, probably London, about 1600, recovered from the Thames foreshore near the Tower

This little pistol is unusual if not unique in that its firing mechanism has survived complete. It is based on French and German wheellock pistols of the late 16th century. The wheellock was an innovative lock mechanism relying on precision manufacturing. It was expensive to produce, and not practical on this scale so the toy is fitted with a simpler matchlock. A glowing piece of slow match is held in the jaws of the lock, and touched into a small powder charge in the pan. The flame runs through the vent – a hole bored into the barrel – and ignites the main charge. IX.5235

Toy pistol, English, probably London, about 1600

These pistols are called 'lemon butt' pistols after the distinctive shape of their butts. This gun was recovered near the White Tower during excavations in the Tower of London in 1956. Sadly it has lost its firing mechanism. XVIII.125

Toy matchlock musket, English, early 17th century

Some of the toy guns were modelled on the standard pattern military musket of the day, shrunk to the same size as the toy pistols. XII.10701

Toy matchlock musket, English, early 17th century
This toy matchlock musket retains its original ramrod screwed into the barrel. This was used to push the powder and shot down the barrel. Made from brass, there was no danger of a stray spark igniting the powder early. Screwing the ramrod into the barrel ensured that it would not get lost (obviously not always successful) and stopped anything from falling down and blocking the barrel. XII.9917

Flintlock toy musket, English, early 19th century
Toy soldiers needed equipment, and this little cast iron musket is just the job. Unlike the earlier brass guns it was never intended to fire, so it has a solid barrel – much safer for children, but still capable of repelling an invading sibling with a telling prod. XII.5160

Flintlock toy gun by James Collins, English, London, about 1830
In the early 18th century there were no specialized toyshops in England, but by the end of the century they had become well established. This full-sized gun appears perfect in every detail, until you look more closely. Close examination of the lock reveals there is no vent. In fact the barrel is solid and made from wood – walnut – and the finish imitates the decorative browning of a metal barrel. It is a very superior boy's toy. It was made by James Collins who advertised his business as 'Goldsmith, Jeweller, Gun and Pistol Repository (successor to Wilson's Gun Repository)'. His shop was on the corner of Vigo Lane and Regent Street in London from 1825–54. XII.4551

Action men

These small armours were the action figures of their time. They are made of steel just like real armours with many plates held together with internal leather straps and rivets. All these miniature armours have fully working parts: the visors of the helmets can be lifted and the limbs can move. They are so realistic that some are good enough to be armourers' models or demonstration pieces for full-sized armours.

Miniature armour, German, 19th century

This is a complete head-to-toe armour for war, but in miniature. It is in the 16th-century style but was probably made in the 19th century. The tiny rivets join the plates together and allow them to move. It even has a lance-rest on the breastplate and its own sword. The 'bellow' visor on the helmet is particularly lovely. II.274

Miniature half-armour, German, about 1590

This miniature half-armour armour shows signs of having been played with and is well worn in parts. As a foot-soldier figure of the 16th century, it does not need any leg-defences. The wooden face and hands were probably added in the 19th century. This is the toy armour shown in the poster for 'The Knight is Young' exhibition. II.273

Miniature armour, probably French, about 1620
This figure is a cuirassier who was a heavy cavalryman in the early 17th century. The cuirassier never had steel lower leg defences but wore leather boots instead. The helmet visor of this toy can be lifted to reveal a humorous face complete with moustache. II.272

Miniature armour, Dutch, about 1630
This armour is also modelled on a cuirassier. The helmet has a delightful embossed flower decoration on it. This armour also has a spare cuirass and a deep collar to wear with a buff coat, so the toy can be dressed as another action figure called an harquebusier, a light cavalryman. II.176

Oriental

Ian Bottomley, Senior Curator of Oriental Arms and Armour

As in Europe, the sons of oriental nobility were educated for the role they were to play in later life. Since many oriental nobles decended from military families, it was natural for the children of those families to be schooled in the martial arts from an early age. It was important that a child became accustomed to handling weapons so that by the time he became adult, his body had developed sufficiently to cope with the stress and fatigue involved in fighting. In many oriental cultures, the carrying of weapons was an outward symbol of rank. It was natural therefore that the sons of nobles were equipped with miniature versions of these same weapons to indicate their status.

India

The Royal Armouries collection is rich in the arms and armour of India, having received shipments of specimens following the Sikh and Afghan wars of the 19th century. Although we have no children's armour from India, we do have several axes and maces that were made for the children of Indian nobles. Despite their size, these are real weapons fully capable of inflicting serious injury.

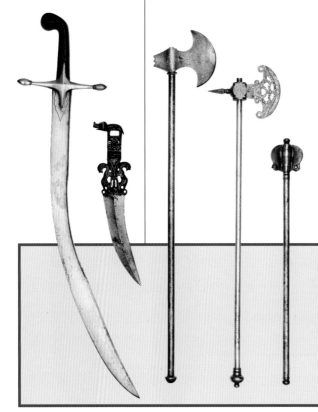

Small weapons

These scaled-down weapons were made, not only to accustom the child to the handling and carrying of weapons, but also as an outward indication of their status.

Mainly Indian, these would be carried by the sons of Maharajahs and other Indian potentates.

Mail shirt, Tibetan, 19th century

This mail shirt is an interesting example that shows how these valuable objects were traded from country to country.

It was discovered in 1904 by Colonel James McCleverty at Jelap-la, the principle pass between Tibet and Sikkim. This type of mail, in which brass and iron links are used to form a pattern, is an Indian tradition where the two colours of the metals are likened to the mixing of the muddy waters of the river Ganges with the darker water of the Jumna. XXVIA.18

Japan

Nowhere were arms and armour venerated more than in Japan. Despite an unbroken succession of emperors, for most of the last thousand years the real power was in the hands of the military class, the buke. This, combined with ancestor worship, ensured that the children of the buke were surrounded by a culture that venerated arms and armour. In this climate, the martial virtues of absolute loyalty to one's lord and prowess in arms were raised to the status of a cult. Around the age of 8, a Japanese boy would cease to be regarded as a child and if of sufficient rank, be given his first sword. Those with considerable wealth might also give the child his first armour as well. By the age of 15, he would be considered old enough to enter the adult world.

▼ *Miniature armour, Japan, 19th century* XXVIA.143

Fifth of May

This was and still is an important date in a Japanese boy's calendar. Paper carp are flown from tall poles to symbolise the hardships the fish meet whilst swimming up-stream, and the similar struggle the boy will experience in life. Indoors, miniature armours, swords, bows and other military equipment are displayed to remind him of his destiny. Dolls representing military heroes set him standards to which he should aspire. Most of the dolls and other equipment are made of wood and paper, but the armour shown here (XXVIA.143) is constructed of russet steel like a real armour. The accurate detailing suggests it was made by a working armourer for a wealthy household.

You may have noticed that girls have not featured much so far. Why not? While brothers and sisters may have worn similar clothes and been educated together in the nursery, when they emerged into the larger world, boys attracted more attention. It was boys who would grow up into fighting men and rulers. It was boys that the educational writers of the Middle Ages concentrated on with only passing reference to girls.

Head girls

Well-bred young ladies would be trained in household management, very basic healthcare and they might learn to read and write. Of course there were exceptions to the rule. Being female did not stop Lady Jane Grey or Princess Elizabeth Tudor, descendants of Henry VII, from receiving an extensive education and being noted for their scholarship. In adult life their experiences were very different.

Jane, a pawn in her family's political ambitions was married young and was declared Queen of England on 10 July 1553. She spent all of her nine-day reign in the Tower of London, and was executed there in 1554, aged 17. Elizabeth too had a stay in the Tower, but finally gained the throne in 1558, ruling until 1603, and giving her name to an era.

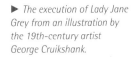

▶ *The execution of Lady Jane Grey from an illustration by the 19th-century artist George Cruikshank.*

▼ Illustration from La Vie des Femmes Célèbres, French school, Musée Dobrée, Nantes/Bridgeman Art Library

Joan of Arc (1412–1431)

In times of emergency wives defended family castles, and may even have worn armour as they did so. One of the few girls we do know who donned armour and went to war was Joan of Arc.

Directed by heavenly voices, the teenaged Joan led the French to victory over the English – raising the siege of Orleans and leading the advance to Rheims. She was captured by the Burgundians in May 1430 and sold to the English for 10,000 livres. Condemned to death by the Bishop of Beauvais for witchcraft and heresy, she was burnt at the stake at Rouen in 1431. Her crime was as much not conforming to the accepted ideas of ladylike behaviour and beating the boys at their own game as any religious fault. She was finally canonized in 1920.

The thrill of the chaste!

Undoubtedly sisters tried on their brother's armours and learnt to master arms, but they did so quietly. It was not considered 'ladylike' or a skill that would be useful in the hunt for a husband. Nevertheless some wealthy women owned fine crossbows and guns, and enjoyed hunting. Fourteen-year-old Margaret Tudor,

sister of Henry VIII, stopped off at Alnwick in 1503 on the way to her first marriage to James IV of Scotland. Here the Duke of Northumberland entertained her with a day's hunting, and she shot a buck. Her niece Elizabeth was famous for her love of the chase.

Annie got her gun!

Annie Oakley embarked on her sharp-shooting career through economic necessity. As a young girl in Darke County, Ohio, she learnt to shoot wild animals. The story goes that if she shot them through the eye, their undamaged skins could be sold for more. She went on to make her name with Buffalo Bill's Wild West Show touring America and Europe from 1885 –1902.

◄ *Girls just wanna have fun! It is extremely rare to find an illustration of a girl playing with weapons. We like to think that this little girl has borrowed her brother's hobby horse and toy lance.*
Detail from the Concert at the Fountain tapestry, French school. Musée des Gobelins, Paris/Bridgeman Art Library

▼ *The Young Archers by George Hay*
These girls are indulging in the more sedate pursuit of target archery. Considered suitable for young ladies in the 18th and 19th centuries, it was one of the few sports unhampered by long skirts.
Courtesy of Julian Simon Fine Art Limited/Bridgeman Art Library

◄ *A lithograph by A Hoen, dated 1893, showing Annie Oakley wearing a few of the many dozens of shooting medals that she won in her lifetime.* Buffalo Bill Historical Centre

Further reading

Aries, P 1962 *Centuries of childhood.* London, Jonathan Cape

Blackmore, H L *Elizabethan toy guns.* 6th Park Lane Arms Fair Guide: 10-13

Blair, C 1972 *European armour.* London, B T Batsford

Cunningham, H 1995 *Children and childhood in Western society since 1500.* London, Longman Studies in Modern History

Cunnington, P and A Buck 1965 *Children's costume in England 1300-1900.* London, Adam and Charles Black

Fraser, A 1979 *King Charles II, his life and times.* London, Weidenfeld and Nicolson

Hibbert, C 1968 *Charles I.* London, Weidenfeld and Nicolson (Penguin 2001)

Jordan , W K (ed.) 1966 *The chronicles and political papers of King Edward VI.* London, Allen & Unwin

Loach, J 1999 *Edward VI.* London, Yale University Press

Norman, AVB 1980 *The Rapier and the small-sword 1460-1870.* London, Arms and Armour Press

Orme, N 1984 *From Childhood to chivalry – the education of the English kings and aristocracy from 1066-1530.* London, Methuen

Orme, N 2001, *Medieval children.* London, Yale University Press

Sotheby's 1988, *Childhood.* Catalogue of the Loan Exhibition of Works of Art.

Strong, R 1986 *Henry Prince of Wales and England's lost renaissance.* London, Thames and Hudson

Royal Armouries Museum
Armouries Drive
Leeds. LS10 1LT

© 2003 The Trustees of the Armouries
First published 2003
Series Editor: Debbie Wurr
Series Designer: Geraldine Mead
Designer: Graham Moores
Series Photographer: Rod Joyce

ISBN 0 948092 54 8

Printed in Great Britain